JESSIE RITTENHOUSE

A Centenary Memoir-Anthology

Jessie B. Rittenhouse

Jessie Rittenhouse

A Centenary Memoir-Anthology

MARGARET WIDDEMER

South Brunswick and New York
A. S. Barnes and Company
for the
POETRY SOCIETY OF AMERICA

© 1969 by The Poetry Society of America
First Edition

THE CENTENARY SERIES

Added volumes in this series will appear on the occasion of the 100th anniversary of the birth of distinguished past members of The Poetry Society of America. The memoir-anthology on *George Sterling* by Charles Angoff also appears in 1969.

The general editor of the Series is Gustav Davidson.

Library of Congress Catalogue Card Number: 77–76165

A. S. Barnes and Co., Inc.
Cranbury, N.J. 08512

SBN 498–07452–8
Printed in the United States of America

CONTENTS

Jessie Rittenhouse: A Centenary Memoir-Anthology   9

A Letter or Two   31

A Selection from Jessie Rittenhouse's Lyrics   37

JESSIE RITTENHOUSE

Jessie Rittenhouse:
A Centenary Memoir-Anthology

IT is not primarily because of her poetry that Jessie Rittenhouse is remembered.

She was quite frank about her verse. She knew it was not great. She had no vanity. What she did have was clear sight, excellent evaluating capacity, a brilliant critical ability, and executive ability coupled with selflessness. And she wrote and worked in a period when poetry could be simple, could be rhymed and quiet and sincere, could be learned by heart or carried around in a billfold. It could even be something that helped you over a hard spot.

There may still be people—there were once a good many —who carried around or tucked into their handbags one poem she wrote. "My Wage," it was called. It began, "I bargained with Life for a Penny." There may have been more, in that day. But the thing Jessie made wasn't, as I said, primarily poetry.

There is a tablet, or it may be a plaque or only an inscription—I have never seen it—in St. Paul's Cathedral in London. Its subject does not have a statue or a graciously carved memorial. It is dedicated to Christopher Wren: and the words of it are:

"*Si monumentum requiris, circumspice.* If you would see his monument, look around you." For Christopher Wren's monument is the Cathedral itself, which he made.

The same words might be said of a lesser creator. For the Poetry Society of America, which has been a center of culture, and of encouragement to poets and poetry, for sixty-seven years, is in a sense the monument to a dedicated woman, Jessie Rittenhouse.

She was in middle life when I knew her first: a courageous little driving person of incredible faith and courage and cheerfulness. She was the executive secretary of the Poetry Society; but she was more than that. What she said later of Bliss Carman, then in the front rank of American poets, could be said of her:

"(His poetry began) a gesture of release . . . one of the returnings to freedom and simplicity." It was, in England, the period of *The Yellow Book*, a drive toward decadence: of Beardsley, Wilde; a trend which was the tail end of the aesthetic movement: which was mocked at by Gilbert and Sullivan's comic operas; but taken seriously, could lead to public shock and disapproval and jail. And Jessie, sworn to courage and affirmation and simplicity, wakened an interest in the creation of poetry, which had flagged in England and had been almost unstirred in America.

She was born in an innocent and hopeful time. There were other women like her in those days, brilliant and courageous and hard driving. It was the time when women were awaking to the fact that they were people, when they desired to change the world for the better, to have the vote, to straighten out the world. Her story is that of other girls of her time. They sound like Louisa M. Alcott heroines. Perhaps they were.

Jessie's is the story of one of these girls. She made high grades in school and college. She made the best of all help given her. She led her classes, she was trailed by the boys, and she picked up a capacity for public speaking at her debating club, and for article-writing in her English courses.

She was like her generation in her enthusiasm for causes. She wanted poetry to be reborn and better known. She also wanted the prisons, which then needed it badly, to be reformed. But even her persistence ended more than once in blind alleys, with this cause. The doors would half-open, then inevitably close.

Not so with writing, however. The doors opened, and stayed open. But Jessie had to earn her own living, and free-lancing, at first, was too precarious. In those days, unless you wanted to be a milliner, only one profession was safe and easy to come by: teaching. So she taught at a private school in Cairo, Illinois: well and successfully, but under the iron and spinsterly hand of a lady who disliked men and believed all teachers should.

Jessie was a leader type, even if she did like men: she stood the nunlike atmosphere as briefly as she could and, after some difficulties, found a more congenial place, and one nearer both her home in Michigan and the city of Chicago. It was an Episcopal school, only an hour from Grand Rapids and a day from Cheboygan, where her mother and her mother's clan lived.

She was nearly as young as the girls she taught—and finally almost too popular with them. They preferred her twenty-three year old chaperonage to that of the older teachers, and the principal couldn't understand girls liking her unless the reason was that she was lax in discipline. There was also a severe theologian at the school's head, who felt that his teachers should think exactly as he did— and he had made up a creed of his own.

But it was not altogether bad. Her year at Akeley had been prefaced by a leisurely view of the first Chicago World's Fair. Her uncles, who were contractors, had prepared the grounds and had put up many of the buildings. Chicago was on the way to her home on Mullet Lake, near Cheboygan, Michigan. Her second year of teaching began. She was a good and inspiring teacher and her pupils remembered her always as stimulating them and opening doors to successful studies.

But teaching was not for her. Frankly, she did not like it—its rules and confines. Again she desired to turn to prison reform. Then it was that the door to her true metier opened once more—and stayed open.

One of the clan of maternal aunts had an adopted daughter, and she asked Jessie to act as her tutor. It was a job which gave her every chance to write on her own: indeed, the aunt encouraged it. And Jessie found herself successfully writing feature articles, preferably about people in the arts, and reviewing modern American poetry.

This was the middle nineties. And poetry, on both sides of the Atlantic, was in the trough which seems to come at every great era's ending. The great American Victorians, though still ranking high, as well as the English, were gone. Their successors were what Edmund Clarence Stedman, whose Victorian and American Anthologies are still classics, called the Gentlemen: charming, urbane men and women whose poems had grace and feeling and wit. But the great winds that had swept them to eminence had died down. Thomas Bailey Aldrich; Stedman himself; Austin Dobson; Calverley the humorist; a score of other such both here and in England.

It was the day of the rondeau, the ballade, the sestina—all the gracefully patterned French forms. They had wit, charm and manner: not strength or greatness. Such of the English who were not still absorbed in Browning and Tennyson, Longfellow and Whittier, and their contemporaries of the Victorian day, were not interested in poetry at all. As a historical fact, this seems odd. The legend always was that England, our cultural source, could never let the torch drop. But facts proved otherwise. The Americans, oddly, were—perhaps languishing a little behind—more interested in poetry than their old mentor.

One cannot say how movements arise. Things are in the air, come in on a wave. But Jessie Rittenhouse, thwarted gently but immutably every time she was drawn toward working for prison reform, was pushed in the direction of next importance to her. She had always been a poetry-lover. Now, after two years of teaching and a little article-writing (and who knows how much private poetry-writing) her face was set, perhaps by fate, perhaps also by inclination, in the perfect position for the work she was to do.

Jessie, staying with the aunt who encouraged her, with sufficient leisure from the tutoring of the young adoptive cousin, with adequate income, went on toward her destined goal.

She knew already that she was talented as a lecturer. She had learned that fiction was not for her. She knew that she was good at article-writing. And throughout her life she felt that something within her guided and steered her way. "I have always found my intuition," she says somewhere, "an infallible guide."

What was the next thing, then? Articles. She did one on St. Augustine, Florida, where she had gone with her aunt. It sold. Another on Minnie Maddern Fiske, then one of the best known actresses, dropped into her lap. Mrs. Fiske was visiting Grand Rapids, and her manager saw to it that Jessie sat by her at a dinner party.

She went on from there: Jessie usually did go on from there. Her good will, her bright charm, friendliness, her Scottish determination and Quaker persistence always seemed to give her entree. The basis of her two passions—prison reform and poetry—was perhaps a drive for making things go somewhere and develop. Now that prison reform was out, poetry was in and was everything. She had read poetry avidly ever since she knew how to read, which, in her day, literate parents taught their children early. She read it and loved it and memorized it as all poets and poetry lovers are bound to do. So it was not long before the passion for human betterment and the passion for poetry fused.

One of those impasses, which with Jessie were usually stepping-stones, now arose. Her mother became seriously ill. Her mother's numerous and prosperous clan had settled into the West some time before. The old family farm belonging to her father in northern New York was inconvenient for ministry to an invalid. So Jessie's father, finally, as there seemed no possibility of his wife's returning to it with him, sold the old farm near Genesee, and bought another near his wife's people. Jessie, to the best of her knowledge, was trapped there, for it was too far from any urban center to offer her chances for articles. In fact, there was nothing to write articles about.

But there was always poetry. Yet everyone told her that love and enthusiasm for poetry made one a dreamer incapable of fitting into the world of successful everyday life. Forgotten was that successful, hardworking playwright named Shakespeare, or Oliver Cromwell's publicity agent, an equally hardworking political writer named Milton. Forgotten, if ever remembered.

So it was in great discouragement that Jessie, wandering among pines near a little woodland lake, met a lady with a book in her hand. She was one of the summer people from a little resort nearby. Jessie had seen her and knew who she was, but had not spoken to her. She came over to Jessie and spoke.

"This is a new book of verse by my cousin Clinton Scollard," she said. "Would you be interested in looking it over?"

When I came, years later, to know Jessie personally, she told me more of that moment.

"When I sat down in the wood to read that book," she said, "I determined that if poetry as fine as this could be so little known, something had to be done, and I made up my mind to do it."

Her work as reviewer and her mission to poetry were thus miraculously fused.

With the prompt practicality which always drove her enthusiasms, she wrote to the author, asking for his picture and some personal data. The cousin who had unwittingly acted as *dea ex machina* willingly gave his address. Scollard was at that time professor of English at Hamilton College. He wrote back, giving her what she asked. While she awaited his reply she went ahead with the review. The critical matter, as she explained, had to be built into the feature article. She sent the article to *The Buffalo Express,* which promptly published it in its Sunday edition.

She was launched. In fact she was launched in more ways

Caricatures of six of the leading poets in the Rittenhouse circle.

than she knew. Perhaps this is not the place to note that she eventually acquired the singer as well as the song: it happened much later. But happen it did. She had no idea of anything like this at the moment. It was sufficient that Clinton Scollard's publishers saw the article, and promptly sent her other books of poetry to review: Alice Brown's *Road to Castaly,* and Hovey and Carman's then or soon to be published *Roads to Vagabondia.* Other publishers did the same.

Jessie went on with a series of sketches of poets and poetry for *The Express* and *The Rochester Union,* the other newspaper to which she had sold some of her first interviews. Her Scottish prudence did not desert her: neither did the backing of her mother's clan, the Macarthurs, thick on the ground there. The uncle and aunt with whom she had spent most of her childhood were in Rochester now. She made up her mind to become an actual reporter. She went to *The Rochester Democrat's* city editor and offered to work for nothing until she had proved herself. She was living, a welcome guest, with her relations. She seemed to surprise the editor. But all he said was, "Give me your address and phone number. I'll call you if anything comes up."

It sounds like the modern formula, "Don't call me, I'll call you." But Mr. Buell, the editor, did call her the very next day. And he sent her to interview Simon Adler, Felix Adler's brother, who was lecturing on what was a very important topic in those days before women's suffrage, "Laws Affecting Women in the State of New York."

She wrote her interview. She also borrowed, by her editor's order (to keep them from anybody else), Adler's original lecture notes. Her article, strongly on the human side, was published without change. We have forgotten what laws did to women in those days. They had no rights over their property or their children.

It was the start of a set of Jessie's interviews with the great suffrage figures of that day: Susan B. Anthony, May Wright Sewell, Anna Howard Shaw, Frances Willard. She made friends with them all; they liked her, and were grateful for what she was doing and what she said about them and their cause.

She went on free-lancing to Chicago. Poetry still, prose authors—crowning the whole edifice with three columns on the great William Jennings Bryan.

But poetry was still what mattered to her most. And it was in Boston that poetry was most alive, most coming. It was there the poets converged, and encouragement for them.

So she went to Boston. She did not plunge in without a life-preserver or two. On the way to Boston she stopped off at Buffalo. She wanted to—and did—see Joseph Hall of *The Buffalo Courier,* who had taken a good many of her articles. He took her to a theater party and a luncheon—both, of course, for interviewable celebrities. It did not take much persuasion on her part—Jessie was always good at persuasion—to elicit a commission for an article on prominent literary Bostonians every other Sunday. And Mr. Hall threw in, without being asked, a suggestion coupled with a promise of free passes for articles about theaters and theater people. He also offered her a letter to the McClure Syndicate, which would have meant steady and well-paid employment and a name. But she did not want to be a newspaper woman. She held to her purpose of writing about poetry and poets for books and magazines.

Settled in Boston, after a brief struggle with finances, the city seemed to open its literary arms to her. Louise Chandler Moulton, then one of the best known women poets and who lived round the corner from her, became her close friend. At Mrs. Moulton's Fridays she met practically every celebrity in the city. And Boston in 1900 was the United States' literary Mecca. The list of Jessie's friends is the list of the litterateurs of that day: Alice Brown, Mary E. Wilkins, Thomas Wentworth Higginson, J. T. Trowbridge, Thomas Bailey Aldrich, Margaret Deland, Kate Douglas Wiggin, Julia Ward Howe: the list is unending.

So far, it was not too lucrative. One morning, after a moment when it had almost seemed necessary to give up, she woke with a new, clear, distinct plan in her mind. Jessie had one of the most useful subconscious minds I have ever known. And, almost hidden by a brisk mid-Western simplicity and friendliness, she was a scholar. Her subconscious mind pointed out to her that she was to edit something much needed and wanted and never before done. It was to be a new one-volume edition of Omar Khayyam, then in the first flush of popularity through the Fitzgerald translation. It was much needed and never before done. But the volume was to comprise, besides the Edward Fitzgerald translations, revisions of even better translations by other men not as yet known in the United States. The edifice was to be, and was, crowned by a collation of the various manuscripts by a well-known Persian scholar named Whitfield. His translation, while not especially fine poetry, adhered to the originals as Fitzgerald had not pretended to do. It was a day of scholars and scholarship. It was certain that the edition would not only be a needed, but a popular, book. There was only one more doubt. Who would publish such a book, whose editor was a young woman who was only known as a clever writer for newspapers?

But her subconscious did not fail her. She woke next morning with her way clear. Little Brown, here in Boston, had liked Jessie's article on the then famous Lilian Whiting sufficiently to make a brochure of it. Paying attention, as usual, to her inner monitor, Jessie promptly called on the publishers. She reminded them of the brochure. One of the principal editors heard her attentively, discussed the Omar Khayyam book with her, and gave his approval.

The book was contracted for, compiled and edited, and it succeeded. Jessie accepted a lump sum for it: she would have done much better to have demanded a contract on a royalty basis. But she was content. She needed the cash, and was not regretful.

She had become an accepted critic of poetry.

She next went to work on the book which was to establish her reputation as a major critic: *The Younger American Poets*. They were the poets of the nineties, Ridgely Torrence, Edwin Arlington Robinson, Edith Thomas, Percy Mackaye, Anna Hempstead Branch and a few others. These were the young men and women who bridged the gap between the great Victorians and the movement called, later, the Poetic Renaissance of America. This was to witness the giant split between Traditionalist and Modernist forces—the changing ideas awakened around 1910 by Freud and, a little later, Joyce, based actually on the ideas of the French Symbolist movement and, in their turn (ironically enough) rooted in Poe and Whitman.

After a summer abroad and a needed rest from the work on her book, she tackled poetic New York and conquered it.

Even in 1905, *The New York Times' Literary Review* was outstanding. Mr. Dithmar, then its editor, had not only himself reviewed her *The Younger American Poets,* but had honored it with an editorial. Jessie went straight to him. Small, alert, bright (and, at 36 Jessie still looked and felt like a girl), there was no question now of her being chosen merely for capacity and personality. She was the Jessie Rittenhouse whose *Younger American Poets* was a book nobody else had thought of writing, and which was a literary necessity. She was a discoverer. She had put the fact that valid and important poetry was being written in America on the map. Mr. Dithmar, on interviewing her, gave her the freedom of his poetry shelf, and, what was better yet, used her untrammeled judgment in choosing who and what were worthwhile in contemporary poetry.

She went to *The Times* once a week and took her choice of the American poetry being published, together with a lesser amount of English poetry. (It was a day when English poetry, whether because its public was tenaciously Victorian or because there wasn't any, was at its lowest ebb.) The era of *The Yellow Book* was fading, if not over. For the moment, it had no successors.

At about this time Theodore Roosevelt, a genuine lover of poetry, discovered Edwin Arlington Robinson. So had Jessie. Madison Cawein, nearly forgotten today but then a leading American poet, introduced Jessie to Bliss Carman, famous also then, and to Ridgely Torrence and Robinson. The last three were then all living at the Judson on Washington Square.

The gentlemen all liked Jessie. People usually did. They did not in the least mind, even Robinson, being discovered by her. But Robinson, as Jessie wrote her mother, was far from delighted at Roosevelt's discovery of not only his poetry but his poverty, which the President promptly remedied by a job in the Custom House with a good salary. The countrywide publicity which followed Roosevelt's own article about Robinson's greatness as a poet, and the knowledge that he had been discovered as what legend described as a ticket taker on the Elevated, and given the Custom House job, distracted Robinson severely. He walked the floor of his room, Jessie said, exclaiming "I shall never live it down! I shall never live it down!"

But he did.

Jessie was on equally intimate terms with all the poets well known then, friend as well as reviewer. It was a time of lyricists: Lizette Woodworth Reese, Charles Hanson Towne, George Sterling, Mary Austin, the visiting Le Gallienne, many others. Poetry had become alive again, known, earnestly read and talked about.

So two lovers of poetry, Mr. and Mrs. Isaac Rice, somewhere about this time, conceived the idea of a salon in New York where poets and lovers of the arts could meet and read and discuss.

Jessie was of course a well-known critic. She was also, though that gift had lain silent for a time, a born organizer. St. Ignatius once remarked that you could get anything in the world done if you only let other people have the credit for it. Whether or not Jessie had heard this statement repeated, she usually acted on it. She was one of the committee deputized to deliberate on the plan. She reported to the group that this was too big an idea to confine to a single private salon. If anything, it should be nationwide and have a public meeting-place. Dr. Edward J. Wheeler, the editor of the influential magazine *Current*

Literature, agreed with her, and added that as director of the National Arts Club on Gramercy Square he could assure the group harbor, as the Poetry Society of America, in their gallery.

The Rices, naturally, didn't like the idea of having their Poetry Salon transformed into even so important a thing as a Poetry Society of America, and removed from the salon to the National Arts Club. But the committee had already evolved its clearcut and completed plan, down to the name, scheme and aforesaid place of meeting. This they presented on the spot to the assembled company—and the assembled company agreed. Dr. Wheeler was elected president, Jessie secretary; fifty leading poets were asked to become charter members. So, of course, were the Rices—but they never came near the Society to the day of their demise.

The first meeting was nevertheless held at the National Arts Club in October, 1910.

It was a day when poetry was still considered a little odd, not to say humorous, by the less literate general public. Poets were slightly queer. So important a poet as Ridgely Torrence, indeed, put all his powers into arguing Jessie out of being the Society's secretary. It would jeopardize her standing as a major critic, he pleaded, to be publicly affiliated with a body sure to be ridiculed.

And ridiculed it was. It was called the Poets' Union. It was written up by amused reporters in a dozen humorous ways. But it went marching on. So did Jessie Rittenhouse as its secretary, her Covenanter blood holding her staunchly to what she felt—rightly—would be a serious and important and much-needed organization. It was a sacrifice of time and strength. The executive secretary of any organization does most of the actual work. Jessie's own writing—prose and poetry—had to be neglected.

But the Society flourished. The well-known poets joined it, came, contributed and discussed. And whatever the reporters said about it, it proved to be a good, and successful affair. Indeed, in her memoirs Jessie speaks of an early meeting which, unknown to the poets, foreshadowed the two branches of poetry which had scarcely budded yet.

Sara Teasdale, just beginning to write, had come to hear the title poem of her first book, *Helen of Troy,* read. And just behind her sat Ezra Pound, making his first and last visit to the Society, for, as he stated with his usual flair for publicity, he could no longer bear the brunt of America, and was sailing for what proved to be his spiritual home, Italy. (He stopped over in England for a little while, dropped in on France, where I first met him, and eventually, during the 1920's, settled down into the arms of Mussolini and Marinetti, where he learned his artistic creed.)

The branches of the Poetry Society spread. Today there are offshoots in almost every state in the union. As for the New York mother Poetry Society, it became sound, prospering and well-known throughout the world. The English poets, young then, flooded over. They spoke at the annual dinners—Yeats, Masefield, Noyes, de la Mare, Sassoon, A.E., Dunsany—a little wistfully. The English had, they said, compared to the Americans, only a lukewarm interest in poetry. For here in America it was beginning to matter. In England, as Wilfrid Gibson remarked, "they invite me to dinner and praise my work, but they never read it!" The Americans were *reading* poetry.

It was the Poetry Society, around 1918–19, in the person of Jessie Rittenhouse, which wakened the Pulitzer Committee to the need for a prize for poetry. The first was awarded to Sara Teasdale, the Poetry Society volunteering to share the award money. After the second year of the prize—which I have occasion to recall, because I shared it with Carl Sandburg—the Pulitzer Committee took it over entirely, and has continued it to this day.

I had known Jessie personally, I think, about a year when this happened, of course through the Society. She *was* the Society. She must then have been around fifty, though one never thought of her being any age. She was one of those people who do not change.

I had not been in New York or a member of the Poetry Society very long. Poetry had been something one did secretly and did not talk about—at least not unless people found it in magazines and talked first. So the Society and its secretary were a revelation. Jessie's warmth, her friendly enthusiasms, which I suppose years of dealing with shy young poets had built to a gift, were all a delightful surprise. She was as happy as if the award had been given to herself, when she called me from New York to tell me that morning in Larchmont that Mr. Sandburg and I were having the Pulitzer Prize for poetry divided between us.

I don't think any awards for poetry ever came her way. Hers were delicate, quiet, sincere lyrics. People said they were derivative of those of her close friend Sara Teasdale. But I don't think so. People of one period are apt to write alike—they do it still—but the personality behind the poems was her own. The best of them, the one which women still keep in their desks and men in their billfolds, *My Wage* (see anthology section), came as a good many good poems do come, without much conscious volition. While she waited for a friend somewhere, it wrote itself.

It isn't today's poetry; it isn't great poetry. But it has meant a great deal to a great many people. And I think that is all she would have asked for it.

She had written poetry as a young girl; and nearly dropped it because of her work in the years between. But in 1917, caught, perhaps, in the creative wave rising at that time, she began again. Two slim volumes, *The Door of Dreams* and *The Lifted Cup*, were issued within a few years thereafter, published and widely read. Later yet a third, *The Secret Bird* (the title is Swinburne's), followed.

It was her anthologies which made her famous. They are collectors' items now. Her nearly unconscious flair for the needed thing, and the moment to produce it, hadn't failed her. The last standard anthology of American poetry, since Bryant's monumental *Library of Poetry and Song*, was Edmund Clarence Stedman's *American Anthology*, nearly a generation old.

She compiled *The Little Book of Modern Verse* in 1917 and followed it by *The Second Book of Modern Verse* in 1919. Eight years lay between this and *The Third Book of Modern Verse,* published in 1927. The books were done, not chronologically (though, indeed, so many of us had "burst out singing together" that there could have been little of that) but with mood leading to mood. They were successes. The sales on the first of the three books were over a hundred thousand copies. The two that followed earned little less. Joyce Kilmer, reviewing them for *The Times Literary Review,* said "They raised anthology-making to a fine art."

It was no more than the truth. No anthology exists today which has not chosen the poems of forgotten poets. But the three books Jessie collected have perhaps less of these than most. And whether forgotten or not, it is amazing how completely Jessie guessed right as to lasting poetic values.

Another thing, interesting at least, is the fact that *The Third Little Book,* printed in 1927, has so many names valid forty years later: Macleish, Sandburg, John Hall Wheelock, Marianne Moore, T. S. Eliot, Langston Hughes, Ezra Pound, Robert Nathan, E. A. Robinson, Louis Untermeyer, Mark Van Doren, William Carlos Williams, Elinor Wylie—to cull only a few. Indeed, there are few of the poems she chose whose writers are not remembered. And indeed, it would be an act of grace and a very needed one if some intelligent publisher reprinted in one volume so excellent a collection of that high tide of poetry, the 'teens and 'twenties.

From the time of the anthologies, Jessie's life was a super-busy one: lecture tour after lecture tour, book-reviewing in all the leading newspapers and magazines, and for ten years of this the secretaryship of the Poetry Society of America, which in itself (I speak from the experience of a less crowded time) was a big whole-time job. The annual dinners of the Society became more and more important affairs; the leading poets of other countries were glad to be summoned to them. And there was a characteristically Jessie-like affair which preceded them. Jessie gave *her* poetry party.

Who but Jessie would have placidly and brightly welcomed the leading poets of the civilized world in a box of an apartment, with no help to speak of, an octogenarian aunt and mother beaming on the sofa, and chocolate and cookies for all refreshments? It was old America at its best, homely and warm and incredibly crowded, Tight-packed, it welcomed equally and happily the great Europeans of the craft and the shy young newcomers from our far West and South and East. And they were all at ease and enjoying it. It was her idea—and it worked—that our poets should have a chance to meet and make friends with their poets. By the time the actual dinner began, everybody had had time to meet, know one another, be friends. Jessie had a gift for that. (By some strange coincidence, the Society's current Executive Secretary, Charles A. Wagner, lives in the same building on the Columbia campus, 106 Morningside Drive.)

To Jessie's pre-annual dinner parties at Seth Low Hall came trooping Witter Bynner, Vachel Lindsay, Sara Teasdale, Joyce and Aline Kilmer, Edwin Markham and Ridgely Torrence. It was said that William Rose Benet and Elinor Wylie met there (they were later married) and in the goodly company of poets consorting with poets could be found Edwin Arlington Robinson, Cale Young Rice, Olive Tilford Dargan (a charter member of the Poetry Society), Edith Thomas, Josephine Preston Peabody, Robert Frost and Percy MacKaye.

There was a rumor that Jessie practiced what was then known as New Thought. It was a religion which believed that if we built in our minds a picture of what we wanted to receive, it would draw itself to us. Whether or not Jessie practiced it, most of what she wished for, hoped for, and desired, came to her sooner or later, sometimes naturally, sometimes what might seem magically.

Her career had been marked out for her, long ago, when,

wandering in deep discouragement near that little Western woodland lake, the lady came out of nowhere to her with a book in her hand; the lady she had seen but did not know. The lady had said out of a clear sky "This is a book of poems by my cousin Clinton Scollard," and gave it to her to read. And Jessie sat down in the wood and read the book, and it made her decide to spend her life in her mission to poetry. She had never met Clinton Scollard: she reviewed the book; his publisher and other publishers sent her his and other books to write about and, as I have said earlier, she was launched.

As of the present, she was fifty-four—if such as Jessie have any age—when she married the man whose poetry had made her resolve in girlhood, "If such poetry as his could be little known, something had to be done and she would do it."

She had corresponded with him then, and since then. But so she had and did always with many other poets. She had a gift of friendliness. How much or how little of a friendship it was, how it moved into being a happy marriage in 1923, I do not know; and, oddly, her poems give us little key. There were love-poems; but in those days that was what everybody still wrote unashamedly. Lyric poetry deals with romantic love. Most poetry, then, was lyric. Also, people who do not fall in love from time to time aren't normal, and Jessie was normal. There is sincerity in her love-poems. But there is a side to poets' work which most people rather prefer to forget. They may write from a springboard of actuality, but they also write quite as convincingly about loves and incidents they have only imagined. (One of Emily Bronte's greatest and most passionate poems had its genesis in one of the child-books the sisters wrote about their dream-world and its dream-hero.) One may guess that Jessie's last little collection of poems, *The Secret Bird,* had a good deal of Clinton Scollard in it. Its lyrics were collected in 1929, after their marriage had run happily for six years.

Clinton Scollard's health could not stand the northern

winters of his ancestral home near Kent, in Connecticut; so, almost from the beginning of their life together, they spent the winters in Winter Park, Florida. It could have been a barren sort of retreat, after New York and its crowd of poets and its old friendships. But Jessie's luck, or rather her life-pattern, held.

A year after the Scollards' arrival, Hamilton Holt took over the presidency of Rollins College, and made it a haven for the arts, poetry in especial. Poets and other writers drifted there. Jessie continued to live as she had at home. Inevitably, she gave courses in poetry: as inevitably she founded the flourishing Poetry Society of Florida, and swept northern friends into her circle. Hers was a warm, hospitable house; she was always writing us alluringly about coming down and letting her arrange readings, or just coming. Most of us did, sooner or later. She made a sort of Magna Graecia of poetry there, an echo of the days before the Depression that changed the old America's heart.

But "nothing that is fair can stay." After nine years of happy marriage, happy surroundings, happy work, an aftermath which made up bountifully for the late harvest, a year came when everything happened at once.

Jessie's mother, whose health had demanded so long ago pulling up the family roots and resettling in Michigan, lived with the Scollards, a nonagenarian now. She died of old age, silently and peacefully. The Scollards were not yet gone from the old Connecticut house where the summers were spent. And that October, without warning, Clinton Scollard's heart condition became serious. In a month more he was gone.

Jessie's closest woman friend, among her many close friends, was the poet Sara Teasdale: that Sara whose beautiful traditionalist lyrics have never gone out of print. Jessie, always courageous, had returned to Winter Park after Clinton's death. It had become a second home: all her ties and arrangements were there. The strain she had been through with her mother and husband was too much for even her buoyant temperament and strong body: she became very ill.

It was a long illness: she was scarcely recovered from it when Sara came to stay with her over the Christmas holidays.

Sara was always physically frail. The gay and charming side that she turned to her friends had another mood beneath it: a melancholy that, as she grew older and less well, came close to melancholia. She had never, actually, been a well woman: she laid it to having been a seven-months' child. And unlike Jessie, who deliberately held herself to health of mind and body, Sara had no will to be well. Indeed, so Jessie told me, Sara believed deeply that if she attained good health it would invalidate her poetic gift. She had always been petted and cared for by everyone near her. She had divorced an unwilling and devoted husband, as she herself told me, because she knew herself unable to carry on a normal pattern of living.

"She told me, when she came to stay with me, that she didn't feel able to talk to anyone," Jessie told me, when, the following Spring, a lecture trip took me to Winter Park. "But she asked me to go on seeing my friends through the holidays. She lay in bed in the room next the living room, and asked to have her door left ajar so that she could hear and see them and enjoy their pleasure."

Sara grew increasingly weak, increasingly hyper-sensitive. Jessie felt that she ought to keep her beyond the planned duration of her visit. But the doctor, who had attended Jessie herself in her own illness, forbade it.

"She is going to commit suicide," he told Jessie forthrightly. "Nothing you can do or say will stop her. And if you ask her to stay with you longer, instead of returning to New York as she has planned, she will do it here. After all you have been through, and your own serious illness, the strain of having it happen in your house is likely to kill you. You must let her go when she wants to."

Sara herself insisted on going.

"So I let her go," Jessie said. "I, too, knew it was bound to come." She had made an attempt on their last trip abroad together.

A little time after her return, Sara quietly took her own

life, peacefully sleeping herself away. The news shocked Jessie into further illness. But her vitality saw her through.

She lived fourteen years longer. She was in her eightieth year when she died. Her courage, her work, her friendships, went on until her death. The Florida Poetry Society, which she had founded as, to all intents, she had the *Poetry Society of America* that was based in New York, went prosperously on. I quote from a letter of Mrs. Willard Wattles: Willard, a known poet of her time and after, lived with his family near the Scollards. They were among her closest friends.

"Jessie never gave up having the Poetry Society meeting. She had founded the Poetry Society, which was very popular . . . it was widely attended, and it was there that Jessie always gave a fine talk. . . . She *was* the Poetry Society of Florida. . . . She was much loved, because she was always kindly, interested in all those about her . . . the manager of the Hearthstone, where she lived after her husband's death, said that she was an asset to the place, not only because she was interesting and well known, but because she never had other than kindly words to say about everyone, which was true. She was a wonderful friend to Willard and me . . . she was gallant, kind and good."

Mr. and Mrs. Wattles were among the last people to see her in her last illness, before she went west to be with her nieces. Her niece, Mrs. Harrigan, whom I remember as Nellie Rittenhouse, flew to Florida in June, 1948, and took her to Grosse Point, Michigan, where, two days after she was placed in the hospital there, she had a final stroke. She died in October of the same year, near her girlhood home in Cheboygan, among her own people.

"Gallant, kind, and good." Perhaps these are not qualities popular or primarily considered today among the arts. But perhaps even so, when coupled as Jessie's qualities were coupled with brilliant critical ability always stimulating and creative—with the ability, of which she herself said little, to waken creativity in the poets she worked with, and to give them the self-belief the poetic temperament needs more than most others, they were great.

From Vachel Lindsay and Joyce Kilmer to that Amy Lowell whose tongue was as sharp as her mind, their words of her are the same: ". . . her devoted work for poetry and her sympathy for poets cannot be sufficiently praised . . ." ". . . a true poet, a just critic, a faithful friend . . . kindest to see and know."

A Letter or Two

TO Nathan Haskell Dole.
1904
My dear Mr. Dole:

To trouble you once again, will you be so very kind as to finish out the address and drop in a postbox for me. I am writing Mr. Powell for a copyright privilege on one or two of his quatrains, to use in my Lovers' Rubaiyat, and cannot for the life of me remember who issued them. You doubtless have the volume and can address him care the publisher. If I were in Boston I could look it up at the Library, but I am in exile in Providence, where his work is not to be found. I shall be more than grateful if you will find out the address and drop it in the nearest postbox at your convenience, and I am always

Very sincerely yours

Jessie B Rittenhouse
333 Laurel Hill Ave, Providence,
March 10, 1904.

To Margaret Widdemer
Winter Park, Fla   C 1929
Dearest Margaret:

How dear of you! In fact, I never knew anyone to take such an interest in an unknown little admirer. You must not feel however, that you must keep this up. Louise is now a young lady of 22, has graduated from the University of Michigan, and has entered upon her second year of teaching

English in a high school in Detroit. She is as pretty as a picture and the most charming young girl imaginable.

You would love each other at sight. She may come to Kent this summer, and if she does I shall have you come out and meet her and my older niece, equally charming. Both girls were with us a few days last summer, having motored out in their own car, but as Clinton was sick I did not do anything for them.

Louise would be charmed, of course, to have your book, but I do feel now that you ought not to take the extra time and expense upon yourself. She must buy your books now, as she is earning a good salary. The girls are going abroad this summer. I tell them it is now or never, as they might get married at any time. They have many admirers.

We came down here as usual in late November, and mother took the flu on the train and was very sick, almost pneumonia. She has recovered but is weak yet, and I have to keep a nurse constantly for her. Clinton is fine, has entirely recovered from his illness of last summer and is golfing daily.

I go to Rollins College twice a week to conduct a poetry course, otherwise I am free and have taken up again the book, mostly autobiographical, that I began several years ago and laid aside when mother was so ill. I hope now to get a mood and finish it.

I have the Poetry Society of Florida still and it has grown till it is the leading thing here. Our meetings put those in New York to shame, or at least some of them do. (Should love to have you send us something to read. We enjoyed the things you sent us a year ago. Something of yours might take the prize.)

How I wish you could come down again this winter. The Mackayes are just across the street from us. Percy is giving a course here on drama for the winter school. We have moved into a lovely large house in another part of town, down near the beautiful Brewer place.

Robert Herrick is here this winter and Mary Aldis is coming. Our literary colony is growing.

The weather is glorious, just tang enough to be stimulating. Yesterday we were in white but today is cool.

Now, my dear, I must stop. I am so rushed. It is a joy to hear from you. I love the collected edition. It must be a satisfaction to have the poems together in that way, and the new ones are among your best.

No end of love always from
Jessie.

Jan 12th.

TO JULIA COOLEY ALTROCCHI. Feb. 14, 1938
Dear Julia:

It was so nice to hear from you. I had the pleasure of meeting Professor and Mrs. Kutz of Berkeley when I first came to Carmel, and they told me of you and your husband, and the very fine work he is doing at Berkeley, and of course I knew of your work and the fine recognition it has had. I am so happy about it.

I came out here to Carmel, really fleeing from my overfull life at Winter Park, Florida, to do some poetry of my own, and also to work on a prose book. Mr. Scollard and I were married out here fifteen years ago, and I was so anxious to come back and relive all those beautiful associations, but I had no idea that such a flood of poetry would come from it as did come to me after I reached here. I have not written anything, scarcely, since he died, but at last that numbness of my heart was unfrozen, and since I left Winter Park in early December, I mave written about fifty lyrics. Of course not all of them pertain to my association with Clinton, but the finer ones do. I have sent the book to Houghton Mifflin under the title, "Golden Fire," and hope that it will be out in the early Autumn.

Now I am working upon a prose book of reminiscences of the poets of my time, those that I did not bring into my autobiography, "My House of Life," published in 1934. You may have seen it.

On this hinges my coming to Berkeley. I would greatly love to come and really cannot say no when my close friends are involved and so gracious as to want me, but if you also have a May dinner I would much prefer to come then, as it would not break into my work as much as it would to stop it for several days in April. Of the two dates you give me, I will take the second, the April 7th, but if you do have a May meeting please let me come then, as it will be nearing my leaving time and will not break especially into my work. You can let me know about this at your leisure. Hildegarde (Hildegarde Hawthorne) is one of my dear old friends. I saw her last Fall in Detroit and we had tea together, Harold Lamb and his wife I also know: Ruth's mother was a well-known friend of many literary folk who used to gather at their apartment. Thereby hangs quite a tale. I doubt whether Ruth is wholly in sympathy with her mother who has grown rather odd of late years.

Of course George Sterling was a very old and dear friend of both Clinton and myself. I see his ghost everywhere in Carmel, though he had gone from here before we came. We saw him at intervals in San Francisco.

What change in all the world of poetry! So many are gone. Last night I went through Sara Teasdale's Collected Work, and almost every poem was known to me in its personal inspiration. I knew by whom it was inspired, the circumstances. I helped her put most of her books together. It was like opening a grave. She nearly died in my house in Florida as she had come down to spend the winter with me, the year that Clinton died, but she was herself in such a dangerous state mentally that finally her nurse and the doctors decided she must go North, and they expected to place her temporarily in a sanitarium for nervous diseases, but she circumvented them. I will tell you more about it when I see you. There are many tragedies in connection with recent years in poetry, such as Vachel's and hers.

Are you interested in the Elinor Wylie fellowship? They are urging me to form a group on the Coast, but Elinor's personal life makes it hard to raise so large a sum to endow a fellowship in her honor than it would if it were some other poet, though this ought not to make a difference, she was such an undoubted genius.

It will be the greatest delight to me to see you and Professor Altrocchi again. I would plan to come up from here one day, stay a day and return the next, say come up on the sixth and return the eighth, if that would be convenient for you. I should be most happy to meet any of the old friends again, or any friends of yours. As I say, if you do have a May meeting, that would suit me better, but I will come in April if you do not.

So, many happy remembrances to you both.
      Affectionately yours
       Jessie B Rittenhouse.
La Playa Hotel Feb 13th, 38th.

A Selection from Jessie Rittenhouse's Lyrics

My Wage

I bargained with life for a penny,
   And Life would pay no more,
However I begged at evening
   When I counted my scanty store:

For Life is a just employer,
   He gives you what you ask,
But once you have set the wages,
   Why, you must bear the task.

I worked for a menial's hire,
   Only to find, dismayed,
That any wage I had asked of Life,
   Life would have paid.

Paradox

I went out to the woods today
   To hide away from you,
From you, a thousand miles away,
   But you came, too.

And yet the old dull thought would stay
   And all my heart benumb—
If you were but a mile away
   You would not come.

Debt

My debt to you, Beloved,
 Is one I cannot pay
In any coin of any realm
 On any reckoning day,

For where is he shall figure
 The debt, when all is said,
To one who makes you dream again
 When all the dreams were dead?

Or where is the appraiser
 Who shall the claim compute
Of one who makes you sing again
 When all the songs were mute?

The Ghost

A score of years you had been lying
 In this spot.
Yet I, to whom you were the dearest
 Had seen it not.

And when today, by time emboldened,
 I looked upon the stone,
'Twas not your ghost that stood beside me,
 But my own.

Loss

Once was the need of you
    A pain too great to bear,
And all my heart went calling you
    In work and song and prayer.

But now dull time has brought
    A sadder, stranger lot—
That I should look upon the day
    And find I need you not.

Defeat

All the gifts I did not ask
    Life came and brought to me,
Until I stood amazed before
    Such prodigality.

And yet I failed in my one task,
    In my one enterprise,—
I could not keep the fire alight
    Within your eyes.

Marsh-Grass

I saw the marsh-grass blowing:
    It took me far away,
For I was born where marsh-grass
    Was endlessly at play.

Its ripples were the gladdest thing
    That I could ever see,
So who would think that marsh-grass
    Would bring the tears to me?

Unsung

The songs I have not sung to you
    Will wake me in the night
And hover in the dark like birds
    Whose wings are tipped with light.

Like birds with restless, eager wings
    That quiver for their flight,
The songs I have not sung to you
    Will wake me in the night.

Freedom

Be free of me as any bird
  That circles in the air,
Be free of me as any cloud
  That mountain summits wear,

Be free as any wandering wind
  That blows across the sea,
Be free as any restless wave
  That moves continually

For freed things must tire of flight,
  And restless things must rest,
And all the lonesome winds must drive
  You to my breast!

Values

O Love, could I but take the hours
  That once I spent with thee,
And coin them all in minted gold,
What should I purchase that would hold
  Their worth in joy to me?
Ah, Love—another hour with thee!

The Miracle

They told me miracles had gone
    The way of childish tales
And that to call them back again
    Not any dream avails.

It may be so to duller folk,
    Who do not know like me
How cold gray skies may break to rose
    And thrill with prophecy.

The Snare

    Many birds will fly away
        From the cages that I build,
    Yet if one shall sing and stay
        I have all the joy I willed.

    Many songs are in the air,
        Flitting like evasive birds,
    Ah, if I but one might snare
        In the cage of words.

One Star

One star over the mountains
    Comes earlier than all,
And waits alone in the solemn sky
    Until the darkness fall.

It parts the mist before it
    It sheds a golden light,
It watches while the evening melts
    Into the purple night.

One star over the mountains,
    Eternal and yet new,
One star over the mountains—
    My thought of you.

In the Green Mountains

I dare not look away
    From beauty such as this,
Lest, while my glance should stray
    Some loveliness I miss.

The trees might choose to print
    Their shadow on the lake:
The windless air might glint
    With aspen leaves that shake.

Over the mountains there
   A thin blue vein might drift;
Then in a moment there
   This thin blue veil might lift,

Ah, I must pay good heed
   To beauty such as this,
Lest, in some hour of need,
   Its loveliness I miss.

The Haunted Heart

I am not wholly yours, for I can face
   A world without you in the years to be,
   And think of love that has been given me
By other men, and wear it as a grace:
Yes, even in your arms there is a space
      That yet might widen to infinity,
      And deep within your eyes I still can see
Old memories that I cannot erase.

But let these ghostly tenants of the heart
   Stay on unchallenged through the changing days
      And keep their shadowy leaseholds without fear,
Then if the hour should come when we must part,
   We know that we shall go on haunted ways,
      Each to the end inalienably dear.

The Ghostly Galley

When comes the ghostly galley
    Whose rowers dip the oar
Without a sound to startle us
    Unheeding on the shore—

If they should beckon you aboard
    Before they beckon me
How could I bear the waiting time
    Till I should put to sea?

Unrest

Now I shall know unrest again,
    And all my heart that was so still
Will beat in me like troubled tides
    And urge me to its will.

Now joy, like an ecstatic flame
    Will light the dark about my bed,—
But with the morning I shall know
    That it was pain instead.

Patrins

You know, dear, that the gypsies strew
   Some broken boughs along the way
To mark the trail for one who comes,
   A tardy pilgrim of the day.

And so my songs, that have no worth
   Save that best worth of being true,
Are but as patrins strewn to show
   The way I came in loving you.

The Door of Dreams

I often passed the Door of Dreams
   But never stepped inside,
Though sometimes, with surprise, I saw
   The door was open wide.

I might have gone forever by,
   As I had done before,
But one day, when I passed, I saw
   You standing at the door.

The Lifted Cup

I lift it up again to you,
   This cup you poured for me,
As one before an altar lifts
   The cup of sanctity.

This deep full cup, this holy cup,
   Your lips have touched, and mine,
Is mystical, for you have turned
   The water into wine.

"We Who Give Our Hearts in Spring"

We who give our hearts in Spring
   Putting all the old life by,
We shall start with everything
   Keen and glad beneath the sky.

We shall know the urge of grass
   Parting each detaining clod,
Know the one sweet day they pass—
   Flowers, spirit of the sod.

We are caught into the flame
   Where the golden fire runs,
All its ardor is the same,
   To the flesh and to the suns.

The Altar

Between our lips a ghostly thing
   Escapes and flies on noiseless wing
It is my soul that would not mate
   With your soul at the outer gate
But sought the still and hidden shrine
   Where pale lights burn to the divine,
My soul that could not worship there
   Because it found the altar bare.

The Star

You were aloof as a star in space
   That holds alone its charted way,
You felt the cold and stellar air
   Where winds of heaven play.

But now I know the lonely God
   Who made all things from His desire
Gave to the star the whitest flame
   Because its heart is fire.